Maximize Your Martial Arts Training

The Martial Arts Training Diary

Maximize Your Martial Arts Training

The Martial Arts Training Diary

Turtle Press
Hartford

Dr. Art Brisacher

Maximize Your Martial Arts Training: The Martial Arts Training Diary

To contact the author or order additional copies of this book:

Turtle Press
401 Silas Deane Hwy.
PO Box 290206
Wethersfield, CT 06129-0206
1-800-778-8785

Back Cover Photo by Phil Williams
Special thanks to Millie See

Library of Congress Card Catalog Number 96-610
ISBN   1-880336-09-X
First Edition, Second Printing

Library of Congress Cataloguing in Publication Data

Birsacher, Art, 1952 -
   Maximize your martial arts training : the martial arts training
diary / Art Brisacher. -- 1st ed
      p.   cm.
   Includes bibliographical reference (p.   ).
   ISBN 1-880336-09-X
   1. Martial arts--Training. 2. Diaries.   I. Title.
GV1102.7.T7B75   1996
796.8--dc20   96-6103

Contents

Training Diary # _____

This Diary Belongs To:

_____

Start Date _____

Completion Date _____

ACKNOWLEDGMENTS

Charles Roy Schroeder and Bill Wallace, **KARATE: BASIC CONCEPTS AND SKILLS** (excerpted from pp. 122,123), copyright 1976 by Addison-Wesley Publishing Company, Inc. Reprinted by permission of the publisher. Quotes on pages 150 and 195.

Geroge Seldes, **THE GREAT QUOTATIONS**, copyright 1960, 1966, 1983 by George Seldes. Published by arrangement with Carol Publishing Group. A Citadel Press book. Quotes on pages 189, 190, and 227.

Terence Webster Doyle. **KARATE: THE ART OF EMPTY SELF**, copyright 1989 by Terence Webster Doyle. Reprinted by permission of the Atrium Society. Quotes on pages 109 and 150.

Dan Millman, **THE INNER ATHLETE**, copyright Dan Millman. Reprinted by permission of the Stillpoint Publishing Company. Quote on page 13.

Michael Lynnberg, **WINNING! GREAT COACHES AND ATHLETES SHARE THEIR SECRETS OF SUCCESS**, copyright 1993 by Michael Lynnberg. Quotes on pages 14, 24 and 65.

Dedication

This book is dedicated in memory of my parents, Art and Irene, and with eternal gratitude to my wife Ingrid.

Foreword

This book is designed as a vehicle for all martial artists to help themselves improve and grow during their own personal martial arts journey using the martial art/style of their choice. The sole purpose of this book is to help people at any age, and at any level, maximize their martial arts training and consequently get the most from their martial arts experience.

Never is there any attempt to compare one style of martial art to another style, and never is it suggested that one style or one martial artist is superior to another. Also, when references are made, stories are told, and quotations are used, they are used to motivate and inspire the reader. At no time has an item been selected to promote a particular style or individual.

Lastly, I would like to thank my instructors and our grandmaster. They have all been wonderful teachers and have provided excellent leadership in an outstanding organization. The most difficult task I had when writing this book was omitting references to my own style of martial art since I have great appreciation and admiration for the people involved in our worldwide organization.

Chapter 1

Getting Started

Every athletic career,
no matter how modest or lofty,
is a journey.

- Dan Millman, author of The Warrior Athlete -

I'm very good at inspiring myself,
and my log (training diary)
is one of the most important tools I have.

- Lynn Jennings, 1992 Olympic medalist, 10,000m run -

You don't run twenty-six miles at five minutes a
mile on good looks and a secret recipe.

- Frank Shorter, marathon champion -

Practice without improvement is meaningless.

- Chuck Knox, pro football coach -

You become a champ by fighting one
more round.
When things are tough
you fight one more round.

- James J. Corbett, world champion bare knuckle boxer -

It's lack of faith
that makes people afraid of meeting
challenges, and I believed in myself.

- Muhammad Ali -

Chapter 1
Getting Started

In most aspects of our lives, we want to work smart, not hard, but the vast majority of martial artists I have worked with want to work hard and smart! Keeping a training diary or journal is the way to work smart, and the idea is not new. Training diaries/journals have been used successfully by weight lifters, runners, marathon runners, triathletes and other athletes for years.

Athletes have used training diaries for a long time because it is the best way to work smart! A training diary is the place where athletes record their dreams and goals, and how they intend to accomplish them. Then they monitor their progress and when the day comes, they have a personal record (PR). They know their PR is real because they have it documented in their diary. It could be the first mile they ever ran without stopping, the first marathon they have ever completed, their first 200 pound bench press, or the fact that they lost ten pounds since New Year's Day.

Many athletes consider their training diaries their greatest motivational tool. World records and national records are great but they belong to others. Nothing beats your own personal record being broken because it belongs to you. This is especially true when you are in a healthy productive routine and can see many more personal records coming your way. Now is the time for you to use this powerful motivational tool in your own martial arts training.

What is a martial arts training diary? First and foremost it is a book. It is a martial arts book like no other because it is written by you, about you. It will be both a personal record of your growth and development and a practical training guide. Your hard work and effort should produce the results you desire. Monitoring your efforts with this diary will help you identify what works for you. There is no wrong way to do this. The simple act of thinking about what you are doing is guaranteed to produce a positive change in you.

More importantly, your martial arts training is a journey, maybe the most important, most exciting journey of your life. It is extremely important that you record, document and preserve this wonderful experience in writing. You deserve your martial arts dreams, and working smart combined with working hard is the closest thing you will ever get to a guarantee that you will reach your dreams. If you are to grow as a martial artist, then you must set new goals and challenges for yourself. This book will be your guide.

What is in a martial arts training diary? It is a book that will maximize your martial arts training regardless of your age, experience, level of expertise, or individual style. Keeping this martial arts diary holds tremendous benefits for the new student on his first day of class and for the experienced instructor who has been teaching for twenty years.

Regardless of your particular style or type of martial art, there are some universal aspects to everyone's martial arts journey: you must set goals, monitor your progress, and reflect on your progress. Sparring and forms are also included because the vast majority of styles have sparring or some sort of fighting and forms or some program for regular practice of predetermined sequence of moves.

Using the Diary Pages

The following are brief summaries of the six chapters or areas that are suggested for monitoring: GOALS, PROGRESS CHARTS, FORMS, SPARRING, REFLECTIONS, and NOTES.

Chapter 2: GOALS

A place to record your specific desired achievements. This is where your dreams stop being dreams and start becoming reality. This is the first step of a long wonderful journey.

Chapter 3: PROGRESS CHARTS

A place to record your level of performance for different activities, i.e.. losing weight, running, walking, lifting weights, breaking boards, flexibility, push-ups, class attendance, etc.

Examples of other areas you could monitor:
- body weight
- % of body fat
- general health
- flexibility
- weight training
- time for mile run
- time for doing a specific form
- number of boards for a specific break
- height of a kick
- bench press

Chapter 4: FORMS

For Students: A place to record your instructor's comments, suggestions, corrections, and coaching points for each form. You may wish to record information for this section immediately after class while your instructor's comments are fresh in your mind.

For Instructors: A place to identify major points to stress when teaching a specific form, and a place to list additional resources such as drills and supplementary activities to improve students' proficiency.

Chapter 5: SPARRING

A place to record an opponent's strengths/weaknesses and note your own strengths/weaknesses against that opponent. This is also a section to record instructor's comments and suggestions for improvement on overall technique. A sample entry might include the following: "Mark has a tendency to drop his right hand after he does a right front kick - try a reverse punch after blocking his kick."

Chapter 6: REFLECTIONS

A place to record your thoughts, feelings, reactions, and ideas about any aspect of your martial arts experience.

Chapter 7: NOTES

A place to record any additional information that is important to you. Sample entries could include the following:
- dates and times for classes
- camps and tournaments
- dates of belt tests
- fees collected or paid
- names, addresses, and phone numbers
- attendance
- sequence of teaching specific techniques

Enrichment Topics

These supplements are interspersed throughout the entire training diary. Each is designed as a single panel. They provide information from the following categories:

GENERAL PHYSICAL FITNESS:

This category includes a wide range of physical fitness information:
- ☒ Target heart rates for aerobic training
- ☒ Signs of excessive training
- ☒ Percent of body fat
- ☒ Temperature heat index chart
- ☒ Wind chill factor chart
- ☒ Proper stretching information

SUPPLEMENTAL ACTIVITIES:

This category includes activities that are designed to broaden your horizons. They make you think-feel-experience new situations and, therefore, gain new perspectives and greater insight into the martial arts world and your own life:
- ☒ Read about a martial art or martial artist
- ☒ Learn about a different style
- ☒ Take photographs of yourself doing your martial art
- ☒ Talk about your training with a senior student
- ☒ Research a martial arts topic or problem
- ☒ Go to a tournament
- ☒ Attend a summer camp
- ☒ Workout outside, at the beach, or in the mountains
- ☒ Subscribe to a martial arts magazine

QUOTES:

This category includes informative and inspirational quotations from the following:
- ☒ Martial artists
- ☒ Sports figures
- ☒ Motivational speakers

Topics covered:
- ☒ Martial arts training
- ☒ Fitness training
- ☒ Goal setting
- ☒ Self defense
- ☒ Motivation

TRAINING DEVICES:

This category includes information on how to make various training devices:
- ☒ Makiwara board holder
- ☒ Stretching devices
- ☒ Bag/chin-up bars

MISCELLANEOUS INFORMATION:

This category includes coaching points on the various activities involved with or suggested by this training diary. These helpful hints will be useful for the experienced martial artists and athletes in general.

VIGOROUS EXERCISE = LONGER LIFE

A Harvard study (4/95) that looked at 17,300 middle-aged men for over twenty years, has found that men who engaged in regular vigorous exercise (not non-vigorous, such as golf) had a 25% lower death rate during the study period. The researchers defined vigorous as doing 1,500 calories worth of exercise a week such as jogging or walking briskly for 15 miles a week or the equivalent. Here are some additional examples:

♦ Walking at four to five mile/hour for 45 min. five times a week.

♦ Playing one hour of singles tennis three days a week.

♦ Swimming laps for three hours a week.

♦ Cycling for one hour, four times a week.

♦ Jogging at six to seven miles an hour for three hours a week.

♦ Rollerblading for two and a half hours a week.

MAYBE YOU'RE TOO OLD?

People thought Jim Ward was too old when he accepted a bet and entered a 10k race (6.2 miles) at the age of 64, and maybe Jim thought he was too old because he did finish last in his age group.

But in the last 13 years Jim Ward must have gotten much younger because today he is preparing to run in his fourth consecutive Ironman Triathlon in Hawaii and hoping to improve his record time for the third consecutive year.

To provide perspective, a 10k race is 6.2 miles, a marathon is 26.2 miles, and the Ironman triathlon is like three marathons. It starts with a swimming marathon (2.4 miles), followed by a bike marathon (112 miles), and ends with a running marathon (26.2 miles).

A busy day (or year) by anybody's standard!

Well maybe with any luck you are too old - just like Jim Ward.

Chapter 2

Goals

I feel that the most important step in any major
accomplishment is setting a specific goal.
This enables you to keep your mind focused
on your goal and off the many obstacles that will
arise when you're striving to do your best.

- Kurt Thomas, Olympic gymnast -

Goals are not etched in concrete.
You have to be willing to be flexible and
change your goals if things pop up.

- Steve Scott, American record holder, mile run -

Whatever your goal in life, be proud of every
day that you are able to work in that direction.

- Chris Evert, pro tennis champion -

If a person believes he deserves success,
he's got a shot at it. There's only one way I
know to feel you deserve success, and that's
if you work hard.

- Lou Holtz, Notre Dame football, head coach -

Desire is the most important factor in the
success of any athlete.

- Willie Shoemaker, record setting jockey -

If you don't dream, you may as well be dead.

- George Foreman, heavyweight champion of the world -

Chapter 2
Goals

Goals are extremely important. They are the beacons by which an athlete finds his way. A goal is the point of focus that directs your efforts and decisions. Zig Zigler, an extremely popular motivational speaker, describes a world champion archer who is trying to hit a target using his bow and arrow. The problem is the archer is blindfolded and being spun around in circles. The point is, how can this world champion archer hit a target (goal) he can't even see. Or better yet, how can you hit a target (goal) you don't even have!

There are basically two major categories of goals. First are the goals that are like shooting for the moon. They are grand and they arouse our greatest passions. They make you feel like you are talking with a genie and he is about to grant anything you desire. These goals are what you really want in the grandest sense. These goals are called long-term goals.

The second type of goal is what you are actually willing to do day to day or week to week. These goals are the ones that lead to the long-term goals. For example, if your goal is to complete your first marathon in September 1996, you will have a number of intermediate goals along the way. The first short-term goal may be to run three times a week to start, and the next short-term goal might be to run five days a week with one run being 60 minutes or more. Along the way you may decide that losing weight will be extremely helpful in making the long-term goal of running and in completing the marathon easier to attain. There is no big or great long-term goal that is ever accomplished without a long trail of many smaller intermediate or short-term goals being met along the way.

After planning, setting, and accomplishing many goals for over thirty years, one thing has become perfectly clear. I always intend to go from point A to a point B when trying to accomplish a particular goal. I have never actually made it from A directly to B. Something will always happen and become an obstacle, and you will have to deal with it. Make a plan, expect something to go wrong (because it will!) and then solve the problem and move on. That is how the process works.

In other words, do not dream wonderfully exciting dreams and set good sound serious goals for making your dreams a reality, and then throw everything out the window at the first sign of trouble. Expect trouble, and then attack each problem that presents itself one at a time. I always start at point A and plan to go to point B and always it seems that I must detour through C,D,F,...W,X,Y, and Z to finally get to point B. I have also discovered that the greater personal benefit and growth comes from the detour rather than the direct route. You definitely grow more from the extra challenges and the extra challenges are the most enriching part of the process.

Where should one start when setting personal training goals? I have found reality is a good place to start. Be totally honest with your present situation or condition. Know the facts. It may be depressing to realize you have gained thirty-five pounds since college or high school and you now weigh 230 pounds. But as you move forward and make progress, you will wear the fact that you used to weigh 230 pounds like a badge of courage. One day you'll be telling people how much you have lost and how much you used to weigh. *The more discouraging your starting point looks, the greater your progress will be appreciated when you look back at that horrendous starting point.*

One last word about starting at reality. Many people spend a tremendous amount of physical and emotional energy trying to hold on to the last bit of "fantasy", believing that they are in better shape than they actually are, or that their skill level is a little better than it really is. Relax and let go of any false pride. It is all going to work out great! Get to know the real you. You will find that you have a lot of qualities that you can feel good about, and the greatest source of pride will be the amount you have grown and improved on your own journey of becoming the best martial artist you can be.

Setting your Goals

Page 31 and 32 are show sample pages completed to help you get started. The goal pages for you to fill in begin on page 33. Four important things to remember when you start setting your goals:

1) *Goals should be clearly stated - and in measurable terms.*

When a goal is written properly, anyone could come along and decide objectively if that goal has been accomplished. For example, if your goal is worded, "I want to increase my upper body strength," it would be very difficult to objectively measure whether or not this goal has been accomplished. However, if your goal is worded, "I want to be able to do 10 push-ups," then it will be very easy to decide if you can or cannot do 10 push-ups! Anyone could come by and verify your success or failure.

2) *Have a deadline.*

For many people this is the key to success. Deciding on a goal is something you can do sitting in your favorite chair or lying in bed. It can be done in a fairly inactive state. However, once a deadline is set, your plans are connected to some sort of action, some sort of time line. For example, if my goal is to lose ten pounds, then what does that indicate that I must do today or this week - nothing really. However, if my goal is to lose ten pounds in ten weeks, then my actions have a clearer cause and effect relationship. If I have a goal of losing ten pounds in ten weeks then that means that I should loose one pound each week or 500 calories per day. Now I may exercise more or eat less, but I have something I should do today! If I decide to *pig-out*, then I am making tomorrow more difficult. If I lose three pounds one week then I might want to ease up a little the next week. Day to day decisions and choices are much clearer when a goal has a time frame and a deadline.

3) *Be realistic while still aiming high.*

It is very important to be excited about what you are trying to accomplish. The natural excitement that is present at the start of this process should be used to make it fun and fuel the drive to accomplish your goal. The best way to utilize this initial excitement is to really appreciate the little day to day successes that are needed to get to the great big exciting goals. Know that there is no instant way to accomplish important goals. The only way is one little step each day. Acknowledge and appreciate each little step every day.

4) *Goals must be consistent with your values.*

Goals must be important and exciting to you but also you must believe that what you are doing is right and good. First and foremost, a goal must truly be *your* goal and not one someone else wants or thinks you should have. Morally you should feel good about what you plan to accomplish and how you intend to get there.

SIGNS OF EXCESSIVE TRAINING

- Your **resting pulse rate** (taken first thing in the morning) will begin to **rise.**

- Regular (normal) **soreness** from working out does not go away between workouts.

- **Headaches** and **colds** become more frequent and last longer.

- Difficulty **falling asleep** and **staying asleep** throughout the night.

- Unable to **concentrate.**

- Unusual or excessive **weight loss.**

WEIGHT LIFTING GUIDELINES

Always **warm up** and **stretch** before working out.

If you are using **free weights**, make sure you always lift with a spotter. The spotter should be positioned to safely take the weight from you if you can no longer lift it.

For **strength training**: do exercises with sets of four to eight repetitions (maximum) and do three sets, every other day. **Do not lift with the same muscle groups every day.**

For **endurance** training: do exercises with sets of 12 to 16 repetitions, and do three sets **every other day**.

Exhale as you **lift** the weight and **inhale** as you **return** the weight to the starting position. Always remember - do not hold your breath when lifting.

GOALS

Long term goal: _To enter three tournaments in the next year_

Date completed: _____

Date set	Short-term Goals	Date Completed
May	Learn five new sparring combinations in next 2 months	July
May	Improve stamina so I can spar for 2 minutes by Dec.	
June	Run four miles without stopping	August

GOALS

Long term goal: _To be able to break three boards (3" of wood) with a side kick for black belt test._

Date completed: _____

Date set	Short-term Goals	Date Completed
May	To kick the heavy bag 100 times a week for 12 weeks	September
May	To break one plastic board with a side kick (use shoes) 5 times a week for 3 weeks	June
June	To break 2 plastic boards with a side kick 5 times a week for three weeks	
July	To break 2" of wood	

GOALS

Long term goal:_____

_____

_____

_____

_____

Date completed:_____

Date set	Short-term Goals	Date Completed

GOALS

Long term goal:_____

_____

_____

_____

_____

Date completed:_____

Date set	Short-term Goals	Date Completed

GOALS

Long term goal:_____

_____

_____

_____

_____

Date completed:_____

Date set	Short-term Goals	Date Completed

GOALS

Long term goal:_____

_____

_____

_____

_____

Date completed:_____

Date set	Short-term Goals	Date Completed

GOALS

Long term goal:_____
_____
_____
_____
_____

Date completed:_____

Date set	Short-term Goals	Date Completed

GOALS

Long term goal:_____

_____

_____

_____

Date completed:_____

Date set	Short-term Goals	Date Completed

GOALS

Long term goal:_____

_____

_____

_____

_____

Date completed:_____

Date set	Short-term Goals	Date Completed

GOALS

Long term goal:_____

_____

_____

_____

_____

Date completed:_____

Date set	Short-term Goals	Date Completed

GOALS

Long term goal:_____

_____

_____

_____

_____

Date completed:_____

Date set	Short-term Goals	Date Completed

GOALS

Long term goal:_____

_____

_____

_____

_____

Date completed:_____

Date set	Short-term Goals	Date Completed

GOALS

Long term goal:_____
_____
_____
_____
_____

Date completed:_____

Date set	Short-term Goals	Date Completed

GOALS

Long term goal:_____

_____

_____

_____

_____

Date completed:_____

Date set	Short-term Goals	Date Completed

GOALS

Long term goal: _____

_____

_____

_____

_____

Date completed: _____

Date set	Short-term Goals	Date Completed

GOALS

Long term goal:_____

_____

_____

_____

_____

Date completed:_____

Date set	Short-term Goals	Date Completed

GOALS

Long term goal:_____

_____

_____

_____

_____

Date completed:_____

Date set	Short-term Goals	Date Completed

GOALS

Long term goal:_____

_____

_____

_____

_____

Date completed:_____

Date set	Short-term Goals	Date Completed

GOALS

Long term goal:_____

_____

_____

_____

_____

Date completed:_____

Date set	Short-term Goals	Date Completed

GOALS

Long term goal:_____

_____

_____

_____

_____

Date completed:_____

Date set	Short-term Goals	Date Completed

GOALS

Long term goal:_____

_____

_____

_____

_____

Date completed:_____

Date set	Short-term Goals	Date Completed

GOALS

Long term goal:_____

_____

_____

_____

_____

Date completed:_____

Date set	Short-term Goals	Date Completed

GOALS

Long term goal:_____

_____

_____

_____

_____

Date completed:_____

Date set	Short-term Goals	Date Completed

GOALS

Long term goal:_____

_____

_____

_____

Date completed:_____

Date set	Short-term Goals	Date Completed

GOALS

Long term goal:_____

_____

_____

_____

_____

Date completed:_____

Date set	Short-term Goals	Date Completed

GOALS

Long term goal:_____

_____

_____

_____

_____

Date completed:_____

Date set	Short-term Goals	Date Completed

GOALS

Long term goal:_____

_____

_____

_____

_____

Date completed:_____

Date set	Short-term Goals	Date Completed

_____

_____

_____

_____

_____

_____

_____

_____

_____

_____

_____

_____

_____

_____

GOALS

Long term goal:_____

_____

_____

_____

_____

Date completed:_____

Date set	Short-term Goals	Date Completed

GOALS

Long term goal:_____

_____

_____

_____

_____

Date completed:_____

Date set	Short-term Goals	Date Completed

GOALS

Long term goal:_____

_____

_____

_____

Date completed:_____

Date set	Short-term Goals	Date Completed

GOALS

Long term goal:_____

_____

_____

_____

_____

Date completed:_____

Date set	Short-term Goals	Date Completed

GOALS

Long term goal:_____

_____

_____

_____

_____

Date completed:_____

Date set	Short-term Goals	Date Completed

GOALS

Long term goal:_____

_____

_____

_____

_____

Date completed:_____

Date set	Short-term Goals	Date Completed

GOALS

Long term goal:_____

_____

_____

_____

_____

Date completed:_____

Date set	Short-term Goals	Date Completed

Chapter 3

Progress Charts

Talent is God-given, be humble;
fame is man-given, be thankful;
conceit is self-given, be careful.

- Anonymous (often quoted by John Wooden) -

Chapter 3
Progress Charts

The key in keeping progress charts is that you are consistently measuring the variable you want to measure. For example, your concern is measuring your weight. Let's say your goal is to lose 25 lbs. If your bathroom scale says you weigh 136 lbs., the doctor's scale says you weigh 145 lbs., your friend's scale says you weigh 140 lbs., and this is all on the same day, then you are not getting reliable information. Now if you get on your bathroom scale three times in a row and each time you weigh 136 lbs., then you have a reliable indicator. Your scale may be five pounds off but if it goes up three pounds or down two pounds, at least you know it's a honest change in your body weight.

Another area of concern after finding a reliable measuring device is to eliminate all other variables that might indicate a false reading. When you are looking at your body weight, for example, you do not want different outfits or different types of shoes to change your weight. The idea is to weigh yourself the same time of day under the exact same conditions. You can drop a number of pounds just by having a strenuous workout or going on a long run. The best method is to do it every morning, in the nude, when you first wake up. This way you have eliminated just about every possible variable other than weight gain or loss which is precisely what you wanted to monitor.

Weight loss or weight gain is probably the most common type of self monitoring people get involved with, but athletes tend to do much more, and martial artists are even more specialized in their areas of performance assessment.

Areas of assessment may include strength, flexibility, speed, focus, class attendance, workout frequency, board breaking, tournament performance, belt tests and scores, and camp attendance. Anything you care about can be monitored.

The key to any type of assessment is to make sure you are actually measuring the specific thing you want to measure and that you have a consistent method of measuring the desired trait so that other variables are not being measured instead. The following are some suggested methods for greater consistency and reliability.

WEIGHT:

This is your total body weight under "normal" conditions. Most people use their bathroom scale. For under $100 there are some very accurate and reliable models. Weigh yourself the same time every day wearing the same outfit. Most experts say one or two pounds a week is the most you should expect in either gaining muscle or losing fat. Pick one day a week to do the actual weight that counts. When you get your weight where you want it then you might check it once a month.

STRENGTH:

Strength training is about having more power. This means more power for any sport you might play. To increase muscular strength you must regularly contract the muscle against a slightly greater force than it is used to. Strength can be monitored by looking at the following: push-ups, pull-ups, weight lifting exercises such as bench press, leg presses, curls, etc. When you want to test your strength, it is best to be fresh but warmed-up because you want to make sure you are not checking endurance. It would probably be better to do this at the beginning of a workout rather than the end. Strength improvements seem to come slowly so you may want to measure these monthly or bimonthly.

BODY MEASUREMENTS:

Many body builders and other athletes take precise measurements to determine if their particular exercise program is producing the results they want. For example, if they want to lose three inches off their waist or gain two inches on their arms, they need a way to measure whether their present plan of action is working. If the present plan is not working, they need to switch to something that is working. Again, first thing in the morning is probably the best time of the day to take any measurements in order to eliminate other variables such as your latest meal or a recent workout. It is also helpful to have a training partner or someone to actually do the measurements for you (let's say an unbiased observer).

AEROBIC FITNESS:

Aerobic fitness deals with your cardiovascular endurance, or how well your heart and lungs work. This includes how efficient your arteries, veins, and blood vessels are in conjunction with your heart and lungs. As your heart gets stronger, it will pump more blood throughout your body with each beat. You can increase your cardiovascular fitness in an unlimited number of ways. You can run, walk, jog, swim, row, step, stair climb, skate, hike, or go dancing, as long as you are keeping you heart at 55%-90% of your maximum heart rate. The way you find your maximum heart rate is to start with 220 and subtract your age. For example, if you are 40 then you would take 220 minus 40 to get your maximum heart rate of 180. So when you are exercising aerobically you are keeping your heart between 55%-90% of this maximum number of 180. As an example, an individual who is 40 years of age must exercise at a heart rate between 99-162 beats per minute in order to receive the benefits of exercising aerobically. It is important to note that some experts believe that the 70%-85% range is best for improving your aerobic fitness.

When athletes check out their aerobic fitness, they usually check how far they can go in a predetermined time or how long it takes to travel a predetermined distance. It does not matter if you run, step, bike, stationary bike, row, tread or whatever, but it must take a minimum of twenty minutes. Also, if your aerobic activity is done outdoors, keep in mind other variables that might affect your time or distance such as the wind, heat, humidity, cold, or windchill factor. All of these could provide additional stress that your cardiovascular system must deal with.

FLEXIBILITY:

A joint is considered flexible when the connective tissues and muscle around the joint do not restrict its natural range of motion. In the past, people were considered to have either a flexible or an inflexible body. Now it is believed that a person will have various degrees of flexibility throughout their body. The key to monitoring flexibility is to make sure you are at the state of being warmed up when you test it. How far you can stretch varies tremendously with a warm stretch and a cold stretch. For example, a hot shower can greatly increase your range of motion. The best time to check your flexibility is after a workout, when you are still warm but not necessarily fatigued.

One excellent method for testing the flexibility of your lower back and hamstrings is to sit with your legs on the floor with your feet against a box. Keep your knees straight and lean forward. If you cannot reach the box, then measure how far you are from the box. If you can reach the box, then measure how far you can reach on top of the box. This is a safe, consistent system for monitoring the flexibility of your lower back and hamstrings. If you are monitoring other areas, try to devise other systems that are equally safe and consistent.

BOARD BREAKING:

Board breaking is used primarily to demonstrate the power that a martial artist has when doing a particular move or technique. Most people without martial arts training cannot visualize or appreciate the power that exists when they see a martial artist striking the air or delivering a carefully controlled attack on a training partner. Breaking boards is something that everyone can understand and appreciate.

Boards vary a great deal, so the challenge is to minimize these variables as much as possible. Try to get the same kind of wood, grade of wood, cut to the same dimensions, and maybe even from the same lumber yard. For example, you may use twelve inch by one inch, grade two pine and cut the individual pieces into ten inch sections. Reject any damp, sticky, or sappy wood.   Another variable to consider is the people holding the boards for you when you are attempting to break them. Some people hold the boards very well. They are strong and there is no give when the boards are struck, while other holders might let their arms bend or they may lean back on impact. One way to resolve this problem is to use the same holders each time. Good or bad, having the same holders each time eliminates the variable of the holders. The best way, however, is to use the type of board holder that is supported by a wall. In this case, the only variable that exists is how well you perform your breaking technique.

One final word about keeping your progress charts. There have been a number of areas suggested for monitoring in this chapter. These are only suggested areas. Only you can decide what is important for you! It could be the number of yoga or ballet classes you attend in a year or the number of conferences you attend at which you are one of the guest speakers. Anything that is important to you is worth tracking. It is very unlikely that you will regret putting something in your training diary.

The big regret is always when you fail to record the information that you have deemed important. Either you are too tired or you feel embarrassed because you believe you have had a poor performance. Write it down - be cold hearted - be disciplined! What you have written down is knowledge and you can deal with it. What you do not write down is unknown and you can't deal with the unknown. Sample pages are provided on pages 76 and 77. Your diary pages begin on page 78.

AEROBIC TRAINING

Aerobic exercise is defined by The American College of Sports Medicine as exercise that causes your heart to beat at a range of **55%** to **90%** of your **maximum heart rate**.

Maximum Heart Rate is determined by subtracting your age from 220, for example:

For a 38 year old:

$$\begin{array}{r} 220 \\ -\ 38 \\ \hline 182 \end{array}$$

the maximum heart rate is 182.

Aerobic training heart rate range is determined by multiplying your **maximum heart rate** by **55%** to find the lower limit, and by **90%** to find the upper limit. For example:

For a 38 year old the maximum heart rate is 182, so

$$\begin{array}{r} 182 \\ \times\ .55 \\ \hline 100 \end{array} \qquad \begin{array}{r} 182 \\ \times\ .90 \\ \hline 163 \end{array}$$

the **Aerobic Training Range** is a heart rate between **100** and **163.**

Some experts feel the ideal aerobic training range is **70%** to **85%** of your **maximum heart rate.**

Age	Maximum Heart Rate	Aerobic Training Range	Ideal Rate Range
15	205	112 - 184	143 - 174
20	200	110 - 180	140 - 170
25	195	107 - 175	136 - 165
30	190	104 - 171	133 - 161
35	185	101 - 166	129 - 157
40	180	99 - 162	126 - 153
45	175	96 - 157	122 - 148
50	170	85 - 153	119 - 144
55	165	90 - 148	115 - 140
60	160	88 - 144	112 - 136
65	155	85 - 139	108 - 131
70	150	82 - 135	105 - 127

Heat Index

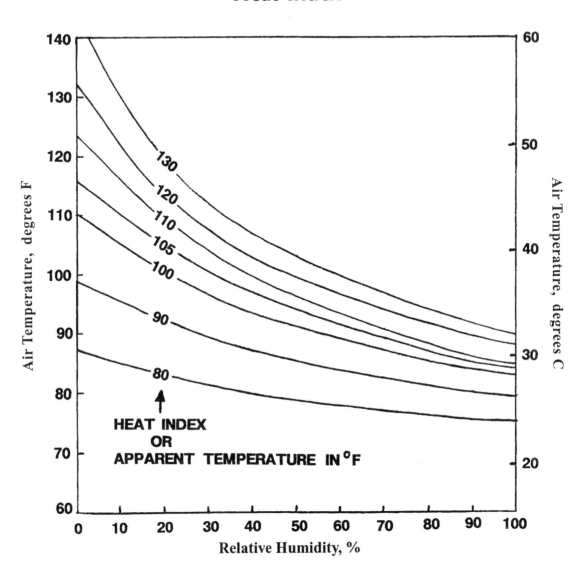

Heat Index	Conditions
80 to 90	Very warm - fatigue possible
90 to 105	Hot - sunstroke, heat cramps and heat exhaustion possible
105 to 130	Very hot - sunstroke, heat cramps or heat exhasution likely, heatstroke possible
130+	Extremely hot - heat or sunstroke highly likely

Wind Chill Index expressed as Equivalent Chill Temperature as used by The National Weather Service

GREAT DANGER — Flesh may freeze within 30 seconds

INCREASING DANGER — Flesh may freeze within one minute

LITTLE DANGER

WIND SPEED (MPH)	\ TEMPERATURE (FARENHEIT) →													
	40	35	30	25	20	15	10	5	0	-5	-10	-15	-20	-25	-30
CALM	40	35	30	25	20	15	10	5	0	-5	-10	-15	-20	-25	-30
5	35	30	25	20	15	10	5	0	-5	-10	-15	-20	-25	-30	-35
10	30	20	15	10	5	0	-10	-15	-20	-25	-35	-40	-45	-50	-60
15	25	15	10	0	-5	-10	-20	-25	-30	-40	-45	-50	-60	-65	-70
20	20	10	5	0	-10	-15	-25	-30	-35	-45	-50	-60	-65	-75	-80
25	15	10	0	-5	-15	-20	-30	-35	-45	-50	-60	-65	-75	-80	-90
30	10	5	0	-10	-20	-25	-30	-40	-50	-55	-65	-70	-80	-85	-95
35	10	5	5	-10	-20	-30	-35	-40	-50	-60	-65	-75	-80	-90	-100
40	10	0	-5	-15	-20	-30	-35	-45	-55	-60	-70	-75	-85	-95	-100

PROGRESS CHART

ACTIVITY: _Running_

Date	Comments
April 15	Ran one block – first run – very tired
April 18	Ran one mile – felt stronger
April 24	Ran two miles – stopped twice
April 28	Ran two and a half miles, felt great
May 8	Ran 3 miles – best yet!

Review your Progress:

Getting much stronger, stamina greatly improved, distance increased

PROGRESS CHART

ACTIVITY: *Push-ups*

Date	Comments
Dec. 2	Can do one push-up, arms feel weak
Dec. 3	did two push-ups, decided to start weight training
Dec. 17	Four push-ups, felt good
Jan. 2	six push-ups, getting stronger
Jan. 14	TEN push-ups! Feels wonderful!

Review your Progress:

Weight training really helped. I feel stronger.
NEXT GOAL: 25 push-ups

PROGRESS CHART

ACTIVITY: _____

_____

Date   Comments

_____

_____

_____

_____

_____

_____

_____

_____

_____

_____

_____

_____

_____

_____

Review your Progress:

PROGRESS CHART

ACTIVITY: _____
_____

Date   Comments

_____
_____
_____
_____
_____
_____
_____
_____
_____
_____
_____
_____
_____
_____

Review your Progress:

PROGRESS CHART

ACTIVITY: _____
_____

Date   Comments

_____
_____
_____
_____
_____
_____
_____
_____
_____
_____
_____
_____
_____
_____

Review your Progress:

PROGRESS CHART

ACTIVITY: _____

_____

Date   **Comments**

_____

_____

_____

_____

_____

_____

_____

_____

_____

_____

_____

_____

_____

_____

Review your Progress:

PROGRESS CHART

ACTIVITY: _____

_____

Date   Comments

_____

_____

_____

_____

_____

_____

_____

_____

_____

_____

_____

_____

_____

Review your Progress:

PROGRESS CHART

ACTIVITY: _____

_____

<u>Date</u>   <u>Comments</u>

_____
_____
_____
_____
_____
_____
_____
_____
_____
_____
_____
_____

Review your Progress:

PROGRESS CHART

ACTIVITY: _____

_____

Date   Comments

_____
_____
_____
_____
_____
_____
_____
_____
_____
_____
_____
_____
_____

Review your Progress:

PROGRESS CHART

ACTIVITY: _____
_____

Date   Comments

_____
_____
_____
_____
_____
_____
_____
_____
_____
_____
_____
_____
_____
_____

Review your Progress:

PROGRESS CHART

ACTIVITY: _____

_____

Date   Comments

_____

_____

_____

_____

_____

_____

_____

_____

_____

_____

_____

_____

_____

Review your Progress:

PROGRESS CHART

ACTIVITY: _____

_____

Date   Comments

_____
_____
_____
_____
_____
_____
_____
_____
_____
_____
_____
_____
_____

Review your Progress:

PROGRESS CHART

ACTIVITY: _____

_____

Date   Comments

_____
_____
_____
_____
_____
_____
_____
_____
_____
_____
_____
_____
_____

Review your Progress:

PROGRESS CHART

ACTIVITY: _____

_____

Date   Comments

_____
_____
_____
_____
_____
_____
_____
_____
_____
_____
_____
_____
_____
_____

Review your Progress:

PROGRESS CHART

ACTIVITY: _____

_____

<u>Date</u>   <u>Comments</u>

_____
_____
_____
_____
_____
_____
_____
_____
_____
_____
_____
_____
_____
_____

Review your Progress:

PROGRESS CHART

ACTIVITY: _____

_____

Date   Comments

_____

_____

_____

_____

_____

_____

_____

_____

_____

_____

_____

_____

_____

_____

Review your Progress:

PROGRESS CHART

ACTIVITY: _____

_____

Date   Comments

_____

_____

_____

_____

_____

_____

_____

_____

_____

_____

_____

_____

_____

_____

Review your Progress:

PROGRESS CHART

ACTIVITY: _____

_____

Date   Comments

_____
_____
_____
_____
_____
_____
_____
_____
_____
_____
_____
_____
_____
_____

Review your Progress:

PROGRESS CHART

ACTIVITY: _____

_____

Date   Comments

_____

_____

_____

_____

_____

_____

_____

_____

_____

_____

_____

_____

Review your Progress:

PROGRESS CHART

ACTIVITY: _____
_____

Date   Comments

_____
_____
_____
_____
_____
_____
_____
_____
_____
_____
_____
_____
_____

Review your Progress:

PROGRESS CHART

ACTIVITY: _____

_____

Date   Comments

_____
_____
_____
_____
_____
_____
_____
_____
_____
_____
_____
_____
_____

Review your Progress:

PROGRESS CHART

ACTIVITY: _____
_____

<u>Date</u>   <u>Comments</u>

_____
_____
_____
_____
_____
_____
_____
_____
_____
_____
_____
_____
_____

Review your Progress:

PROGRESS CHART

ACTIVITY: _____

_____

Date   Comments

_____
_____
_____
_____
_____
_____
_____
_____
_____
_____
_____
_____
_____

Review your Progress:

PROGRESS CHART

ACTIVITY: _____

_____

Date   **Comments**

_____

_____

_____

_____

_____

_____

_____

_____

_____

_____

_____

_____

_____

Review your Progress:

PROGRESS CHART

ACTIVITY: _____

_____

<u>Date</u>   <u>Comments</u>

_____

_____

_____

_____

_____

_____

_____

_____

_____

_____

_____

_____

_____

Review your Progress:

PROGRESS CHART

ACTIVITY: _____

_____

<u>Date</u>   <u>Comments</u>

_____
_____
_____
_____
_____
_____
_____
_____
_____
_____
_____
_____
_____
_____

Review your Progress:

PROGRESS CHART

ACTIVITY: _____

_____

Date   Comments

_____

_____

_____

_____

_____

_____

_____

_____

_____

_____

_____

_____

_____

Review your Progress:

PROGRESS CHART

ACTIVITY: _____

_____

Date   Comments

_____
_____
_____
_____
_____
_____
_____
_____
_____
_____
_____
_____
_____

Review your Progress:

PROGRESS CHART

ACTIVITY: _____

_____

<u>Date</u>   <u>Comments</u>

_____
_____
_____
_____
_____
_____
_____
_____
_____
_____
_____
_____
_____

Review your Progress:

PROGRESS CHART

ACTIVITY: _____

_____

Date   Comments

_____

_____

_____

_____

_____

_____

_____

_____

_____

_____

_____

_____

_____

Review your Progress:

PROGRESS CHART

ACTIVITY: _____

Date   Comments

_____

_____

_____

_____

_____

_____

_____

_____

_____

_____

_____

_____

_____

Review your Progress:

PROGRESS CHART

ACTIVITY: _____

_____

Date   Comments

_____

_____

_____

_____

_____

_____

_____

_____

_____

_____

_____

_____

_____

_____

Review your Progress:

PROGRESS CHART

ACTIVITY: _____

_____

Date   **Comments**

_____

_____

_____

_____

_____

_____

_____

_____

_____

_____

_____

_____

_____

Review your Progress:

Chapter 4

Forms

We practice with full power
because it allows us to go beyond ourselves.
In going beyond ourselves, we go beyond fear;
therefore we are free.

- Terrence Webster-Doyle, Director of the Shuhari Institute -

Chapter 4
Forms

Forms are a predetermined series of movements often including sequences of attacks and blocks directed toward one or more imaginary attackers. For the beginner, forms usually start off fairly simple with basic blocks and attacks. As you advance and move on to higher belts, the forms become more complicated in many ways. The individual moves and techniques become increasingly difficult and then these advanced moves and techniques get put into more complicated combinations of blocks and attacks. Some forms are relatively new and other forms are hundreds of years old. Some forms have only a few moves in the sequence and some may have over 100 movements.

Regardless of your particular style of martial art, there are some aspects of forms training that are common to all martial artists.

1. **You must learn the prescribed movements**. In most cases there is only one correct way to do a movement or the entire form, for that matter.

2. **Pacing or timing must be done correctly**. At times speed is emphasized and at times control is the primary concern.

3. **Strength and power**.

4. **Focus** is the ability to bring together your speed and strength and apply it at a precise point with maximum power.

5. **Balance** is required at all times.

How you achieve these essential elements of your forms training is determined by two important factors: your **instruction** and how you process it, and your **practice** and its effectiveness.

Before you look at yourself and your sources of instruction, it is important to understand the general learning dynamics that take place when learning forms. There are three basic phases to the process of learning forms. The first phase is when you are taking in new information. The second phase is when you are trying to incorporate the new information into the existing frame work of your present knowledge of your martial art. The third phase is when you have incorporated the new information and can perform the movement, the technique, the form, or whatever, by reflex - when you have practiced it to the point where it becomes natural.

Instruction

How do you receive your forms information and process it? Are you getting input from instructors, friends, fellow students, books, videos or other sources? After you receive this new information, how do you implement it into your regular training and practice?

When taking in new information, make sure you understand what you are supposed to be doing and keep in mind your particular learning style. Some people need to have the entire big picture spelled out for them before what they are trying to learn makes any sense to them. Other people need to know move number one and then move number two and so on. If you try to deal with some aspect near the end of the form before the previous sequence of moves is understood, you are just wasting your time because you just will not remember. Be comfortable with your own particular learning style, whatever it is and work with it, not against it.

Training diary entry note: Keep your training diary nearby. If it is acceptable in your particular class and your instructor is   comfortable with it, you might want to write down the   important comments pertaining to your forms while you are in class. Another time people seem to prefer to enter their diary comments is as soon as they return home from class. This is an excellent time because most of the comments will still be fresh in your mind.

Practice

Everyone has their own routine or method of practice, but it is fair to say that everyone puts time and energy into practice because they expect to get better. It is up to YOU to decide what you want from your training and what it means for YOU to get better and improve.

Consistent practice tends to fix most problems. If you are in phase one - trying to get the sequence of moves straight - then the more you do it, the sooner you will get it straight. If you are in phase two - trying to get the separate moves to blend together to become one form - then the more you do it, the sooner it will become smooth. If you are in the third phase - where you can do your form naturally almost without thought - then practice will bring out the best of all five of the previously mentioned elements: accuracy, speed, strength, focus, and balance.

It is important to note that these three phases of learning a form are not mutually exclusive. You may be doing a form that you have been doing for five years and feeling quite natural with it (phase 3) when your instructor points out that you need to improve it in order to perform a specific move with greater strength. As you adjust to this, you may be operating at all three phases. Additionally, as you improve in your forms and become stronger and faster, you will need to make adjustments to accommodate this growth and improvement.

Some of your best questions will come up when you are practicing, and in most cases no one will be around to answer them. This is the time to write questions down in your diary. In general, the notes you take during classes tend to be answers and the notes you take while you are training on your own tend to be questions. A sample diary entry is shown on page 117 and your diary pages begin on page 118.

A Keeper of the Flame

When you are involved with your personal martial arts training program, remember to take care of the most precious aspect of your entire program - your drive - **the flame.** Your drive to improve or your desire to workout and grow as a martial artist is extremely important. Think of this flame as the pilot-light that ignites a powerful furnace. If this pilot-light, this flame, goes out, nothing can happen and everything will shut down. Restarting the flame can take a tremendous amount of energy and it is very difficult to do, at best. Some people never get the flame started again. Be a keeper of the flame. Never let the flame die!

To preserve the flame, keep in mind when making workout decisions that anything you decide to do today is acceptable, as long as it will not make you less excited about your next workout.

Today's training decision should make you more excited about your next workout-not less. Here are some training tips that will help you preserve the flame:

♦   **Don't run too hard, too far, or too fast.**

♦   Don't be too critical about **yourself or your performance.**

♦   **Missing workouts**: Well needed rest is OK, but in most cases it is much better to go to your workout and do less, than it is to miss a workout.

♦   **Watch what you eat and drink.** Always treat yourself as an athlete in training. If you had a $1,000,000 thoroughbred race horse you would take very good care of it. Well, you are many times more valuable.

Leg Stretching Device

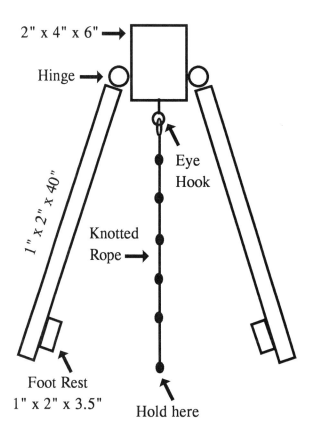

2" x 4" x 6" →

Hinge →

1" x 2" x 40"

Eye
Hook

Knotted
Rope →

Foot Rest
1" x 2" x 3.5"

Hold here

FORMS

Form/belt: *Yellow Belt*

Date *5/21* **Instructor** *Art*

Comments/Notes *increase acceleration – explode into*

each move. Remember – relax, then focus, loose, then tight

Date *6/21* **Instructor** *Debby*

Comments/Notes

Bend front knee more on front stance. Keep fingers tight

together on knife hands.

Date **Instructor**

Comments/Notes

FORMS

Form/belt:_____

Date_____   Instructor _____

Comments/Notes _____
_____
_____
_____
_____

Date_____   Instructor _____

Comments/Notes _____
_____
_____
_____
_____

Date_____   Instructor _____

Comments/Notes _____
_____
_____
_____
_____

FORMS

Form/belt:_____

Date_____   Instructor _____

Comments/Notes _____
_____
_____
_____
_____

Date_____   Instructor _____

Comments/Notes _____
_____
_____
_____
_____

Date_____   Instructor _____

Comments/Notes _____
_____
_____
_____
_____

FORMS

Form/belt:_____

Date_____   Instructor _____

Comments/Notes _____
_____
_____
_____
_____

Date_____   Instructor _____

Comments/Notes _____
_____
_____
_____
_____

Date_____   Instructor _____

Comments/Notes _____
_____
_____
_____
_____

FORMS

Form/belt:_____

Date_____   Instructor _____

Comments/Notes _____
_____
_____
_____
_____

Date_____   Instructor _____

Comments/Notes _____
_____
_____
_____
_____

Date_____   Instructor _____

Comments/Notes _____
_____
_____
_____
_____

FORMS

Form/belt:_____

Date_____   Instructor _____

Comments/Notes _____

_____
_____
_____
_____

Date_____   Instructor _____

Comments/Notes _____

_____
_____
_____
_____

Date_____   Instructor _____

Comments/Notes _____

_____
_____
_____
_____

FORMS

Form/belt:_____

Date_____   Instructor _____

Comments/Notes _____
_____
_____
_____
_____

Date_____   Instructor _____

Comments/Notes _____
_____
_____
_____
_____

Date_____   Instructor _____

Comments/Notes _____
_____
_____
_____
_____

FORMS

Form/belt:_____

Date_____   Instructor _____

Comments/Notes _____
_____
_____
_____
_____

Date_____   Instructor _____

Comments/Notes _____
_____
_____
_____
_____

Date_____   Instructor _____

Comments/Notes _____
_____
_____
_____
_____

FORMS

Form/belt:_____

Date_____   Instructor _____

Comments/Notes _____

_____

_____

_____

_____

Date_____   Instructor _____

Comments/Notes _____

_____

_____

_____

_____

Date_____   Instructor _____

Comments/Notes _____

_____

_____

_____

_____

FORMS

Form/belt:_____

Date_____   Instructor _____

Comments/Notes _____
_____
_____
_____
_____

Date_____   Instructor _____

Comments/Notes _____
_____
_____
_____
_____

Date_____   Instructor _____

Comments/Notes _____
_____
_____
_____
_____

FORMS

Form/belt:_____

Date_____   Instructor _____

Comments/Notes _____

_____

_____

_____

_____

Date_____   Instructor _____

Comments/Notes _____

_____

_____

_____

_____

Date_____   Instructor _____

Comments/Notes _____

_____

_____

_____

_____

FORMS

Form/belt:_____

Date_____   Instructor _____

Comments/Notes _____
_____
_____
_____
_____

Date_____   Instructor _____

Comments/Notes _____
_____
_____
_____
_____

Date_____   Instructor _____

Comments/Notes _____
_____
_____
_____
_____

FORMS

Form/belt:_____

Date_____   Instructor _____

Comments/Notes _____
_____
_____
_____
_____

Date_____   Instructor _____

Comments/Notes _____
_____
_____
_____
_____

Date_____   Instructor _____

Comments/Notes _____
_____
_____
_____
_____

FORMS

Form/belt:_____

Date_____   Instructor _____

Comments/Notes _____

_____

_____

_____

_____

Date_____   Instructor _____

Comments/Notes _____

_____

_____

_____

_____

Date_____   Instructor _____

Comments/Notes _____

_____

_____

_____

_____

FORMS

Form/belt:_____

Date_____   Instructor _____

Comments/Notes _____
_____
_____
_____
_____

Date_____   Instructor _____

Comments/Notes _____
_____
_____
_____
_____

Date_____   Instructor _____

Comments/Notes _____
_____
_____
_____
_____

FORMS

Form/belt:_____

Date_____   Instructor _____

Comments/Notes _____
_____
_____
_____
_____

Date_____   Instructor _____

Comments/Notes _____
_____
_____
_____
_____

Date_____   Instructor _____

Comments/Notes _____
_____
_____
_____
_____

FORMS

Form/belt:_____

Date_____   Instructor _____

Comments/Notes _____
_____
_____
_____
_____

Date_____   Instructor _____

Comments/Notes _____
_____
_____
_____
_____

Date_____   Instructor _____

Comments/Notes _____
_____
_____
_____
_____

FORMS

Form/belt:_____

Date_____   Instructor _____

Comments/Notes _____
_____
_____
_____
_____

Date_____   Instructor _____

Comments/Notes _____
_____
_____
_____
_____

Date_____   Instructor _____

Comments/Notes _____
_____
_____
_____
_____

FORMS

Form/belt:_____

Date_____   Instructor _____

Comments/Notes _____
_____
_____
_____
_____

Date_____   Instructor _____

Comments/Notes _____
_____
_____
_____
_____

Date_____   Instructor _____

Comments/Notes _____
_____
_____
_____
_____

FORMS

Form/belt:_____

Date_____   Instructor _____

Comments/Notes _____
_____
_____
_____
_____

Date_____   Instructor _____

Comments/Notes _____
_____
_____
_____
_____

Date_____   Instructor _____

Comments/Notes _____
_____
_____
_____
_____

FORMS

Form/belt:_____

Date_____   Instructor _____

Comments/Notes _____

_____

_____

_____

_____

Date_____   Instructor _____

Comments/Notes _____

_____

_____

_____

_____

Date_____   Instructor _____

Comments/Notes _____

_____

_____

_____

_____

FORMS

Form/belt:_____

Date_____   Instructor _____

Comments/Notes _____
_____
_____
_____
_____

Date_____   Instructor _____

Comments/Notes _____
_____
_____
_____
_____

Date_____   Instructor _____

Comments/Notes _____
_____
_____
_____
_____

FORMS

Form/belt:_____

Date_____ Instructor _____

Comments/Notes _____

_____

_____

_____

_____

Date_____ Instructor _____

Comments/Notes _____

_____

_____

_____

_____

Date_____ Instructor _____

Comments/Notes _____

_____

_____

_____

_____

FORMS

Form/belt:_____

Date_____   Instructor _____

Comments/Notes _____

_____

_____

_____

_____

Date_____   Instructor _____

Comments/Notes _____

_____

_____

_____

_____

Date_____   Instructor _____

Comments/Notes _____

_____

_____

_____

_____

FORMS

Form/belt:_____

Date_____   Instructor _____

Comments/Notes _____
_____
_____
_____
_____

Date_____   Instructor _____

Comments/Notes _____
_____
_____
_____
_____

Date_____   Instructor _____

Comments/Notes _____
_____
_____
_____
_____

FORMS

Form/belt:_____

Date_____   Instructor _____

Comments/Notes _____

_____

_____

_____

_____

Date_____   Instructor _____

Comments/Notes _____

_____

_____

_____

_____

Date_____   Instructor _____

Comments/Notes _____

_____

_____

_____

_____

FORMS

Form/belt:_____

Date_____   Instructor _____

Comments/Notes _____
_____
_____
_____
_____

Date_____   Instructor _____

Comments/Notes _____
_____
_____
_____
_____

Date_____   Instructor _____

Comments/Notes _____
_____
_____
_____
_____

FORMS

Form/belt:_____

Date_____   Instructor _____

Comments/Notes _____
_____
_____
_____
_____

Date_____   Instructor _____

Comments/Notes _____
_____
_____
_____
_____

Date_____   Instructor _____

Comments/Notes _____
_____
_____
_____
_____

FORMS

Form/belt:_____

Date_____   Instructor _____

Comments/Notes _____

_____

_____

_____

_____

Date_____   Instructor _____

Comments/Notes _____

_____

_____

_____

_____

Date_____   Instructor _____

Comments/Notes _____

_____

_____

_____

_____

FORMS

Form/belt:_____

Date_____ Instructor _____

Comments/Notes _____
_____
_____
_____
_____

Date_____ Instructor _____

Comments/Notes _____
_____
_____
_____
_____

Date_____ Instructor _____

Comments/Notes _____
_____
_____
_____
_____

FORMS

Form/belt:_____

Date_____   Instructor _____

Comments/Notes _____
_____
_____
_____
_____

Date_____   Instructor _____

Comments/Notes _____
_____
_____
_____
_____

Date_____   Instructor _____

Comments/Notes _____
_____
_____
_____
_____

FORMS

Form/belt:_____

Date_____   Instructor _____

Comments/Notes _____
_____
_____
_____
_____

Date_____   Instructor _____

Comments/Notes _____
_____
_____
_____
_____

Date_____   Instructor _____

Comments/Notes _____
_____
_____
_____
_____

Chapter 5

Sparring

The fighter is to always be single-minded
with one object in view - to fight,
looking neither backward nor sideways.
He must get rid of obstructions to his forward
movement, emotionally, physically or intellectually.

- Bruce Lee -

Know the enemy and know yourself, in a hundred battles you will never be in peril. When you are ignorant of the enemy but know yourself, your chances of winning or losing are equal. If ignorant of your enemy and of yourself, you are certain in every battle to be in peril.

- From "Karate-do Kyohan" by Gichin Funakoshi -

(Translated by Tsutomu Oshima)

Training the body in self-defense to know the right thing to do in a threatening situation is essential in ending conflict. If the body doesn't know how to respond properly to a potentially hostile situation, more fear is created and, therefore, a need to defend psychologically. The body needs to know what to do, so it can create a space in which there is no reaction.

- Terrence Webster-Doyle -

In the heat of battle, especially a close contest, you will seldom execute every technique perfectly. However, the more you practice the techniques either individually, in kata movement, or in prearranged sparring, the closer you will come to perfection in freestyle sparring and actual self-defense situations.

- Bill Wallace, Two-time world karate champion -

- Charles R. Schroeder, An exercise physiology specialist. -

Chapter 5
Sparring

There are many different types of sparring used in martial arts training. There are non-contact, light contact, and full contact styles and some schools have a variety of sparring conditions. For example, how you spar when you are training in your regular class workouts may be vastly different than the way you spar when you are in a tournament, and how you spar for a belt promotion test may be different from the way you spar during a public demonstration. Finally, how you respond to a self-defense situation may be drastically different from all the previously mentioned situations.

There are two important areas regarding your sparring that you should keep notes on in your martial arts training diary. First, you should keep notes on the **technical aspects**: attacks, blocks, counters, your strengths and weaknesses, your opponent's strengths and weaknesses. Secondly, you should keep notes on your **personal aspects**: your own emotional and intellectual growth.

Technical Aspects

Technical aspects can be categorized into three areas: the technical perspective, the self perspective, and the opponent's perspective.

The **technical perspective** is just that - a purely technical perspective where the primary focus is on specific moves, such as blocking a kick and doing a reverse punch. For many advanced belts, sparring is just a natural series of actions and reactions that require little if any thought. The greater picture reminds us that it takes many hours of dedicated practice and lots of consensus effort and thought to develop these "natural" reactions.

> *Training Diary Entry Note:* Identify the different techniques that you want to learn, the ones your instructor suggests, the ones other students seem to use so well, and then make a plan to learn and practice these techniques regularly. You will need to keep notes on the learning phase, the practice/drills phase, and then you will need to keep monitoring how the technique is working when you actually spar.

The **self perspective** is where you analyze yourself and your sparring strengths and weaknesses. This should be done in a positive fashion. It should not be done in a way that attacks yourself as a person. For example, "I am a lousy martial artist because my side kick is not so good." or "I am a great martial artist because I can do a great side kick."

You need to approach this self analysis of your sparring in the same way a technician or an auto mechanic would. If something needs work, then fix it. If one technique is not working, replace it with an improved one. Be your toughest critic but more importantly, be your best fan. At no time should your ability or lack of ability to perform a specific technique be confused with your worth as a human being.

The **opponent perspective** is divided into two areas. One area is where you analyze traits and characteristics of all opponents in general. The other area is when you keep very specific notes on individual opponents. This could be the person who beat you in the finals of last year's tournament or maybe the person who seems to always get the best of you in class. When you are looking at your opponents (in general), you are looking to make broad generalizations that will be useful in the vast majority of your sparring matches. For example, you may observe that whenever you try to start off an attack with a really strong side kick, your opponents seem to counter with an attack before you even get started. This would be an extremely important item to note in your training diary. Once you identify the problem, you can begin to work on the solution. You may find that you "telegraph" what you are about to do or maybe you need to work on the speed of your attack. As you become more accustomed to this process of identifying and analyzing these general sparring characteristics, you will also find that one solution will very often solve more than one problem.

Training Diary Entry Note: Keep referring to these general observations because you will need to update and improve them as you become better at seeing yourself and others when sparring.

When you are looking at specific opponents, you can be very specific and you do not need to make generalizations that will apply to everyone. You do, however, need to make sure that your specific observations regarding an opponent are generally true for that particular opponent. For example, if you notice an opponent does a roundhouse kick and then follows with a back spinning side kick it may or may not indicate a pattern. If you see him doing it three or four times in a match and he does it repeatedly in future matches, then you have detected a useful pattern. Another type of observation might be that an opponent starts off very strongly and aggressively but then tends to run out of energy in later rounds.

Training Diary Entry Note: Remember you are looking at a person's general tendencies, and therefore your observations will not be a guarantee that they will follow the exact same pattern every time. Also, keep in mind that people change; they might change bad sparring habits into good sparring habits. Lastly, you might find that every time you spar a particular opponent you can easily get a middle target side kick in on them. If that is working, try something that is not working. In order to improve yourself and grow, you need to work on your weaknesses, not just rely on your strong points.

Personal Aspects

The second area of sparring to monitor is your personal aspects: your own emotional and intellectual growth.

It has been said, "You spar as you are and you are as you spar." Meaning if you tend to be bull headed and just charge into things in your regular daily life, then you probably bull into things when you spar. On the other hand, if you are very timid and afraid to take chances when you spar, you are probably like that in real life.

So if you feel there are characteristics about yourself that you would like to change or improve in your real life, then you might want to work on it in your sparring. The "attitude adjustments" that must take place in order for these changes to occur in sparring are similar to those changes needed in real life.

As you work at your martial art and practice it regularly, you cannot help but grow. These changes will be most evident in how you spar. You start your martial art as a beginner, and months/years later, belts later - you advance. You need to re-examine yourself, because you are not the same person you were when you started. You spar differently because you are different.

A sample diary entry for the sparring pages is provided on page 157 and your diary pages begin on page 158.

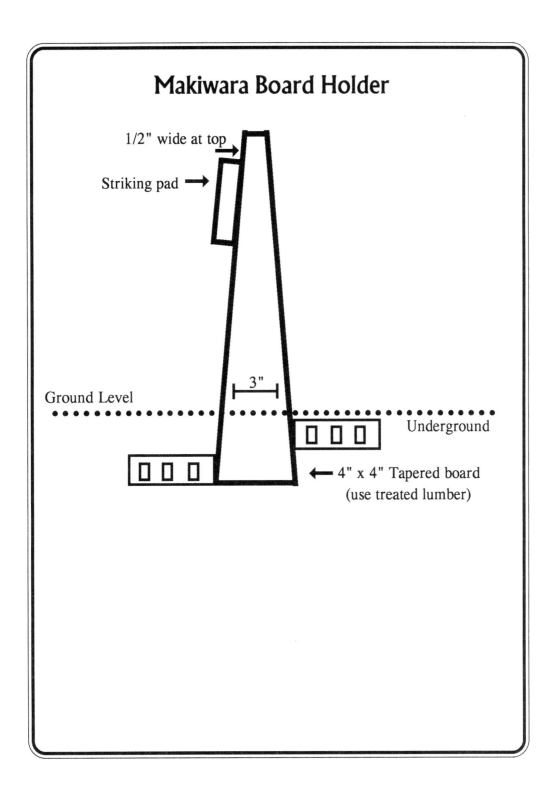

Taking Care of Yourself

♦	Expect some soreness when starting a new activity such as running, weight lifting, or a martial art. Also, expect some soreness when doing a familiar activity but at higher levels of intensity.

♦	If you have a specific area that is sore such as a bruise on your arm or a sore ankle, then you might try giving yourself an ice massage. You need to plan ahead by putting some small styrofoam cups of water into your freezer. When you need an ice massage, take out one of these cups of ice and peel back the styrofoam, leaving enough to hold onto the ice. Then you gently rub the ice onto the sore area.

♦	If the soreness is still bothering you after three days, switch to warm compresses or warm baths. Ice is for the NEW, while warmth is for the OLD.

♦	When you hurt a joint, hand, or foot, you should try to cool it down and elevate the area.

♦	See a doctor if mild pain persists over a week, the pain intensifies or you are worried about the injury. Never underestimate the extent of an injury.

♦	Check with your doctor for the appropriate pain relievers.

♦	Remember when you return to working out after an injury, it will take time to get back to full power. If you miss a month because of a "bad" back, it will take at least a month to return to your normal level of performance (or to get back to where you were previously).

SPARRING

OPPONENT: Janet   **Rank** Brown belt

Date sparred: July 17   **Observations:** I have a tendency to drop my right hand after doing a right front kick.

Advice: Try a reverse punch after blocking the kick.

OPPONENT: Edward   **Rank** Black belt

Date sparred: August 3   **Observations:** Difficult to get a side kick in against Edward

Advice: Try a knife hand to the head to make an opening.

SPARRING

OPPONENT: _____ Rank _____

Date sparred:_____ Observations:_____
_____
_____
_____

Advice: _____
_____
_____
_____

OPPONENT: _____ Rank _____

Date sparred:_____ Observations:_____
_____
_____
_____

Advice: _____
_____
_____
_____

SPARRING

OPPONENT: _____ Rank _____

Date sparred:_____ Observations:_____

_____

_____

_____

Advice: _____

_____

_____

_____

OPPONENT: _____ Rank _____

Date sparred:_____ Observations:_____

_____

_____

_____

Advice: _____

_____

_____

_____

SPARRING

OPPONENT: _____ Rank _____

Date sparred:_____ Observations:_____

_____
_____
_____

Advice: _____

_____
_____
_____

OPPONENT: _____ Rank _____

Date sparred:_____ Observations:_____

_____
_____
_____

Advice: _____

_____
_____
_____

SPARRING

OPPONENT: _____ Rank _____

Date sparred:_____ Observations:_____

_____

_____

_____

Advice: _____

_____

_____

_____

OPPONENT: _____ Rank _____

Date sparred:_____ Observations:_____

_____

_____

_____

Advice: _____

_____

_____

_____

SPARRING

OPPONENT: _____ Rank _____

Date sparred:_____ Observations:_____

_____

_____

_____

Advice: _____

_____

_____

_____

OPPONENT: _____ Rank _____

Date sparred:_____ Observations:_____

_____

_____

_____

Advice: _____

_____

_____

_____

SPARRING

OPPONENT: _____ Rank _____

Date sparred:_____ Observations:_____

_____

_____

_____

Advice: _____

_____

_____

_____

OPPONENT: _____ Rank _____

Date sparred:_____ Observations:_____

_____

_____

_____

Advice: _____

_____

_____

_____

SPARRING

OPPONENT: _____ Rank _____

Date sparred:_____ Observations:_____

_____
_____
_____

Advice: _____

_____
_____
_____

OPPONENT: _____ Rank _____

Date sparred:_____ Observations:_____

_____
_____
_____

Advice: _____

_____
_____
_____

SPARRING

OPPONENT: _____ Rank _____

Date sparred:_____ Observations:_____
_____
_____
_____

Advice: _____
_____
_____
_____

OPPONENT: _____ Rank _____

Date sparred:_____ Observations:_____
_____
_____
_____

Advice: _____
_____
_____
_____

SPARRING

OPPONENT: _____ Rank _____

Date sparred:_____ Observations:_____

_____

_____

_____

Advice: _____

_____

_____

_____

OPPONENT: _____ Rank _____

Date sparred:_____ Observations:_____

_____

_____

_____

Advice: _____

_____

_____

_____

SPARRING

OPPONENT: _____ Rank _____

Date sparred:_____ Observations:_____

_____

_____

_____

Advice: _____

_____

_____

_____

OPPONENT: _____ Rank _____

Date sparred:_____ Observations:_____

_____

_____

_____

Advice: _____

_____

_____

_____

SPARRING

OPPONENT: _____ Rank _____

Date sparred:_____ Observations:_____

_____

_____

_____

Advice: _____

_____

_____

_____

OPPONENT: _____ Rank _____

Date sparred:_____ Observations:_____

_____

_____

_____

Advice: _____

_____

_____

_____

SPARRING

OPPONENT: _____ Rank _____

Date sparred: _____ Observations: _____

_____
_____
_____

Advice: _____

_____
_____
_____

OPPONENT: _____ Rank _____

Date sparred: _____ Observations: _____

_____
_____
_____

Advice: _____

_____
_____
_____

SPARRING

OPPONENT: _____ Rank _____

Date sparred:_____ Observations:_____

_____

_____

_____

Advice: _____

_____

_____

_____

OPPONENT: _____ Rank _____

Date sparred:_____ Observations:_____

_____

_____

_____

Advice: _____

_____

_____

_____

SPARRING

OPPONENT: _____ Rank _____

Date sparred:_____ Observations:_____

_____

_____

_____

Advice: _____

_____

_____

_____

OPPONENT: _____ Rank _____

Date sparred:_____ Observations:_____

_____

_____

_____

Advice: _____

_____

_____

_____

SPARRING

OPPONENT: _____ Rank _____

Date sparred: _____ Observations: _____

_____
_____
_____

Advice: _____

_____
_____
_____

OPPONENT: _____ Rank _____

Date sparred: _____ Observations: _____

_____
_____
_____

Advice: _____

_____
_____
_____

SPARRING

OPPONENT: _____ Rank _____

Date sparred:_____ Observations:_____

_____

_____

_____

Advice: _____

_____

_____

_____

OPPONENT: _____ Rank _____

Date sparred:_____ Observations:_____

_____

_____

_____

Advice: _____

_____

_____

_____

SPARRING

OPPONENT: _____ Rank _____

Date sparred: _____ Observations: _____

_____
_____
_____

Advice: _____
_____
_____
_____

OPPONENT: _____ Rank _____

Date sparred: _____ Observations: _____

_____
_____
_____

Advice: _____
_____
_____
_____

SPARRING

OPPONENT: _____ Rank _____

Date sparred:_____ Observations:_____

_____
_____
_____

Advice: _____

_____
_____
_____

OPPONENT: _____ Rank _____

Date sparred:_____ Observations:_____

_____
_____
_____

Advice: _____

_____
_____
_____

SPARRING

OPPONENT: _____ Rank _____

Date sparred:_____ Observations:_____

_____

_____

_____

Advice: _____

_____

_____

_____

OPPONENT: _____ Rank _____

Date sparred:_____ Observations:_____

_____

_____

_____

Advice: _____

_____

_____

_____

SPARRING

OPPONENT: _____ Rank _____

Date sparred:_____ Observations:_____

_____
_____
_____

Advice: _____

_____
_____
_____

OPPONENT: _____ Rank _____

Date sparred:_____ Observations:_____

_____
_____
_____

Advice: _____

_____
_____
_____

SPARRING

OPPONENT: _____ Rank _____

Date sparred:_____ Observations:_____

_____
_____
_____

Advice: _____

_____
_____
_____

OPPONENT: _____ Rank _____

Date sparred:_____ Observations:_____

_____
_____
_____

Advice: _____

_____
_____
_____

SPARRING

OPPONENT: _____ Rank _____

Date sparred:_____ Observations:_____

_____

_____

_____

Advice: _____

_____

_____

_____

OPPONENT: _____ Rank _____

Date sparred:_____ Observations:_____

_____

_____

_____

Advice: _____

_____

_____

_____

SPARRING

OPPONENT: _____ Rank _____

Date sparred:_____ Observations:_____

_____

_____

_____

Advice: _____

_____

_____

_____

OPPONENT: _____ Rank _____

Date sparred:_____ Observations:_____

_____

_____

_____

Advice: _____

_____

_____

_____

SPARRING

OPPONENT: _____ Rank _____

Date sparred:_____ Observations:_____

_____

_____

_____

Advice: _____

_____

_____

_____

OPPONENT: _____ Rank _____

Date sparred:_____ Observations:_____

_____

_____

_____

Advice: _____

_____

_____

_____

SPARRING

OPPONENT: _____ Rank _____

Date sparred:_____ Observations:_____

_____
_____
_____

Advice: _____

_____
_____
_____

OPPONENT: _____ Rank _____

Date sparred:_____ Observations:_____

_____
_____
_____

Advice: _____

_____
_____
_____

SPARRING

OPPONENT: _____ Rank _____

Date sparred:_____ Observations:_____

_____

_____

_____

Advice: _____

_____

_____

_____

OPPONENT: _____ Rank _____

Date sparred:_____ Observations:_____

_____

_____

_____

Advice: _____

_____

_____

_____

SPARRING

OPPONENT: _____ Rank _____

Date sparred:_____ Observations:_____

_____
_____
_____

Advice: _____

_____
_____
_____

OPPONENT: _____ Rank _____

Date sparred:_____ Observations:_____

_____
_____
_____

Advice: _____

_____
_____
_____

SPARRING

OPPONENT: _____ Rank _____

Date sparred:_____ Observations:_____

_____

_____

_____

Advice: _____

_____

_____

_____

OPPONENT: _____ Rank _____

Date sparred:_____ Observations:_____

_____

_____

_____

Advice: _____

_____

_____

_____

SPARRING

OPPONENT: _____ Rank _____

Date sparred:_____ Observations:_____
_____
_____
_____

Advice: _____
_____
_____
_____

OPPONENT: _____ Rank _____

Date sparred:_____ Observations:_____
_____
_____
_____

Advice: _____
_____
_____
_____

SPARRING

OPPONENT: _____ Rank _____

Date sparred:_____ Observations:_____

_____
_____
_____

Advice: _____
_____
_____
_____

OPPONENT: _____ Rank _____

Date sparred:_____ Observations:_____

_____
_____
_____

Advice: _____
_____
_____
_____

SPARRING

OPPONENT: _____ Rank _____

Date sparred:_____ Observations:_____

_____
_____
_____

Advice: _____

_____
_____
_____

OPPONENT: _____ Rank _____

Date sparred:_____ Observations:_____

_____
_____
_____

Advice: _____

_____
_____
_____

Chapter 6

Reflections

Thinking is the hardest work there is,
which is the probable reason why so few
engage in it.

- Henry Ford (1863-1947) American industrialist -

Let us dare to read, think, speak, and write.

- John Adams (1735-1826) 2ND president of the United States -

There is no expedient to which a man will not go to avoid the real labor of thinking.

- Thomas Alva Edison (1847-1931) American inventor -

Let no man imagine that he has no influence. Whoever he may be, and wherever he may be placed, the man who thinks becomes a light and a power.

- Henry George (1839-1897) American economist -

Thinking leads men to knowledge.
One may see and hear and read and learn as much as he pleases; he will never know any of it except that which he has thought over, that which by thinking he has made the property of his mind. Is it then saying too much if I say that man by thinking only becomes truly great?

- Johann Heinrich Pestalozzi (1746-1827) Swiss educational reformer -

Chapter 6
Reflections

Reflection is taking time out to think about your martial arts training, and equally important, putting your thoughts down in writing in your training diary. How is your training going? Are you making adequate progress? Are you feeling physically stronger? How do you feel about yourself, your training, your classmates, or your friends and relatives? Anything and everything can go into this section of your martial arts training diary.

Remember, this is a martial arts book like no other martial arts book you have ever seen or read before. It is a martial arts book for you, about you, and written by you. One million different martial artists could put entries into their reflections section tonight and no two would be alike. Each person will develop their own unique style of writing, and all styles will be successful. There is no wrong way to do this except to fail to take the time to make the entries. Your martial arts training is only as good as you make it and likewise, your martial arts training diary will only be as good as you make it.

What you decide to think and write about, how and when you decide to actually enter your comments in your martial arts training diary are dictated by your own individual preferences. There are, however, three very broad basic categories of methods that most people fall into with regard to how they decide something needs to be entered into their reflections section of their martial arts training diary.

The three methods of how people decide to make a diary entry are: 1) when a **big or significant event** happens, 2) when a predetermined time is put aside for making **regular diary entries**, and 3) a **combination** of the first and second methods. Here are some pros and cons about these three different categories of entry decisions.

The Big or Significant Event

No one wants to miss recording a big or significant event in their training diary, for example: how you felt the first time you won a match or entered a tournament or how you felt the first time you had to teach a group of lower belt students. The difficult part with this method is many of the really big moments in our lives sneak by us as very small insignificant moments that when looked upon at some future time are found to be monumental turning points.

Here are two examples:

First, there was Al who was an advanced black belt getting ready to break five inches of wood for the very first time. Well, he did it on his very first try; he had no problem at all. Everyone in the class was very excited for him and he was very happy, but days later he came to me with a much greater appreciation of his accomplishment. He told me he was looking back at his training diary where he made an entry years earlier on the day he tried breaking his very first board ... and failed.

He tried four times that day and never did break that one one-inch board, and he hurt his foot on that fourth try because he missed the board and hit the metal board holder. Al was in awe when he realized the amount of progress he had made up to that point in his martial arts training. Obviously, he never would have remembered that rather insignificant day years earlier if he had not made an entry in his training diary.

The second example was Emma. Emma was writing in her training diary the night following the afternoon she received her first degree black belt. She was very proud of herself that day and rightfully so because she earned a black belt, but she told me there was a day two years earlier that she was much prouder of herself. She was sparring a man much larger than she was and he accidently kicked her in the ribs. She really hurt and on her drive home she decided she was definitely going to quit her martial arts training. Later that evening she felt this intense feeling grow within her, a strong resolve that she was not going to quit and if it was the last thing she ever did, she was going to get her black belt. Again the earlier diary note provided the greater perspective of the accomplishment made two years later.

Regular Diary Entries

This method is when you put aside a predetermined amount of time on a regular basis for writing in your martial arts diary. This is the best method by far. You will find that you will sit down to write, thinking you have absolutely nothing to say and then thoughts will just flow on to your paper. It is a process that is very similar to meditating or running or working out. Once you establish the routine things just begin to flow naturally.

The downside of this particular method is that it is extremely difficult to maintain and protect this segment of time from the many demands made upon us in today's fast paced world. When school, work, or the kids are making demands, it seems at times impossible to make time for ourselves. But busy successful people are skilled at managing time and know how to take time for the important things, such as a personal martial arts journey. Consistent diary keeping is a skill to learn and maybe taking five minutes after each martial arts class or workout is the place to start with your reflections. It could be five minutes a day, a week, or a month. It is up to you; the more you put in, the greater your return.

Combination Method

This method is probably the most realistic approach. You set off trying to keep a regular routine of diary entries in your reflections section but, if things happen and you miss some days, it's all right. When the really significant things happen (good or bad, emotional, physical, social, or whatever) you make sure that sooner or later you make a diary entry about that particular event at your earliest convenience.

Just remember that no one looks back years later and says, "Gee, I wrote too much!" Inevitably, everyone wishes they wrote more.

A sample reflections page is provided on page 196 to get you started and your diary pages begin on page 197.

Develop your Craft

To assist the martial artist in remembering the most important principles for improving his craft the following acronym is provided:

C - confidence

R - relaxation

A - ability

F - fitness

T - think

For organizational purposes the above principles have been discussed separately. All are, however, interrelated. Strength in one leads to strength in the others. Confidence, for example, allows one to relax. When relaxed, one can think more clearly. Also, having developed one's skills and physical fitness to a high degree through dedicated training helps to instill confidence.

Charles Roy Schroeder and Bill Wallace, **KARATE: BASIC CONCEPTS AND SKILLS** *(excerpted from p. 123), copyright 1976 by Addison-Wesley Publishing Company, Inc. Reprinted by permission of the publisher.*

REFLECTIONS

Date: _Nov. 5_ **Topic:** _Sparring_

My sparring has improved a lot in 6 months. Sparring William, I defend myself better with blocks and do more hand techniques.

Date: _Dec. 20_ **Topic:** _Stamina_

My stamina has increased a lot. Now I can spar for one minute – a year a go I couldn't even spar for thirty seconds.

Date: _____ **Topic:** _____

Date: _____ **Topic:** _____

REFLECTIONS

Date: _____   Topic: _____

_____

_____

_____

_____

_____

Date: _____   Topic: _____

_____

_____

_____

_____

_____

Date: _____   Topic: _____

_____

_____

_____

_____

_____

Date: _____   Topic: _____

_____

_____

_____

_____

_____

REFLECTIONS

Date: _____ Topic: _____

_____
_____
_____
_____
_____

Date: _____ Topic: _____

_____
_____
_____
_____
_____

Date: _____ Topic: _____

_____
_____
_____
_____
_____

Date: _____ Topic: _____

_____
_____
_____
_____
_____

REFLECTIONS

Date: _____   Topic: _____

_____
_____
_____
_____
_____

Date: _____   Topic: _____

_____
_____
_____
_____
_____

Date: _____   Topic: _____

_____
_____
_____
_____
_____

Date: _____   Topic: _____

_____
_____
_____
_____
_____

REFLECTIONS

Date: _____ Topic: _____

_____
_____
_____
_____
_____

Date: _____ Topic: _____

_____
_____
_____
_____
_____

Date: _____ Topic: _____

_____
_____
_____
_____
_____

Date: _____ Topic: _____

_____
_____
_____
_____
_____

REFLECTIONS

Date: _____ Topic: _____

_____

_____

_____

_____

_____

Date: _____ Topic: _____

_____

_____

_____

_____

_____

Date: _____ Topic: _____

_____

_____

_____

_____

_____

Date: _____ Topic: _____

_____

_____

_____

_____

_____

REFLECTIONS

Date: _____ Topic: _____

_____
_____
_____
_____
_____

Date: _____ Topic: _____

_____
_____
_____
_____
_____

Date: _____ Topic: _____

_____
_____
_____
_____
_____

Date: _____ Topic: _____

_____
_____
_____
_____
_____

REFLECTIONS

Date: _____ Topic: _____

_____

_____

_____

_____

_____

Date: _____ Topic: _____

_____

_____

_____

_____

_____

Date: _____ Topic: _____

_____

_____

_____

_____

_____

Date: _____ Topic: _____

_____

_____

_____

_____

_____

REFLECTIONS

Date: _____   Topic: _____

_____

_____

_____

_____

_____

Date: _____   Topic: _____

_____

_____

_____

_____

_____

Date: _____   Topic: _____

_____

_____

_____

_____

_____

Date: _____   Topic: _____

_____

_____

_____

_____

_____

REFLECTIONS

Date: _____ Topic: _____

_____
_____
_____
_____
_____

Date: _____ Topic: _____

_____
_____
_____
_____
_____

Date: _____ Topic: _____

_____
_____
_____
_____
_____

Date: _____ Topic: _____

_____
_____
_____
_____
_____

REFLECTIONS

Date: _____ Topic: _____

_____

_____

_____

_____

_____

Date: _____ Topic: _____

_____

_____

_____

_____

_____

Date: _____ Topic: _____

_____

_____

_____

_____

_____

Date: _____ Topic: _____

_____

_____

_____

_____

_____

REFLECTIONS

Date: _____ Topic: _____

_____

_____

_____

_____

_____

Date: _____ Topic: _____

_____

_____

_____

_____

_____

Date: _____ Topic: _____

_____

_____

_____

_____

_____

Date: _____ Topic: _____

_____

_____

_____

_____

_____

REFLECTIONS

Date: _____   Topic: _____

_____
_____
_____
_____
_____

Date: _____   Topic: _____

_____
_____
_____
_____
_____

Date: _____   Topic: _____

_____
_____
_____
_____
_____

Date: _____   Topic: _____

_____
_____
_____
_____
_____

REFLECTIONS

Date: _____ Topic: _____

_____
_____
_____
_____
_____

Date: _____ Topic: _____

_____
_____
_____
_____
_____

Date: _____ Topic: _____

_____
_____
_____
_____
_____

Date: _____ Topic: _____

_____
_____
_____
_____
_____

REFLECTIONS

Date: _____ Topic: _____

_____
_____
_____
_____
_____

Date: _____ Topic: _____

_____
_____
_____
_____
_____

Date: _____ Topic: _____

_____
_____
_____
_____
_____

Date: _____ Topic: _____

_____
_____
_____
_____
_____

REFLECTIONS

Date: _____ Topic: _____

_____
_____
_____
_____
_____

Date: _____ Topic: _____

_____
_____
_____
_____
_____

Date: _____ Topic: _____

_____
_____
_____
_____
_____

Date: _____ Topic: _____

_____
_____
_____
_____
_____

REFLECTIONS

Date: _____ Topic: _____

_____
_____
_____
_____
_____

Date: _____ Topic: _____

_____
_____
_____
_____
_____

Date: _____ Topic: _____

_____
_____
_____
_____
_____

Date: _____ Topic: _____

_____
_____
_____
_____
_____

REFLECTIONS

Date: _____ Topic: _____

_____
_____
_____
_____
_____

Date: _____ Topic: _____

_____
_____
_____
_____
_____

Date: _____ Topic: _____

_____
_____
_____
_____
_____

Date: _____ Topic: _____

_____
_____
_____
_____
_____

REFLECTIONS

Date: _____ Topic: _____

_____

_____

_____

_____

_____

Date: _____ Topic: _____

_____

_____

_____

_____

_____

Date: _____ Topic: _____

_____

_____

_____

_____

_____

Date: _____ Topic: _____

_____

_____

_____

_____

_____

REFLECTIONS

Date: _____ Topic: _____

_____
_____
_____
_____
_____

Date: _____ Topic: _____

_____
_____
_____
_____
_____

Date: _____ Topic: _____

_____
_____
_____
_____
_____

Date: _____ Topic: _____

_____
_____
_____
_____
_____

REFLECTIONS

Date: _____ Topic: _____

_____
_____
_____
_____
_____

Date: _____ Topic: _____

_____
_____
_____
_____
_____

Date: _____ Topic: _____

_____
_____
_____
_____
_____

Date: _____ Topic: _____

_____
_____
_____
_____
_____

REFLECTIONS

Date: _____ Topic: _____

_____
_____
_____
_____
_____

Date: _____ Topic: _____

_____
_____
_____
_____
_____

Date: _____ Topic: _____

_____
_____
_____
_____
_____

Date: _____ Topic: _____

_____
_____
_____
_____
_____

REFLECTIONS

Date: _____ Topic: _____

_____

_____

_____

_____

_____

Date: _____ Topic: _____

_____

_____

_____

_____

_____

Date: _____ Topic: _____

_____

_____

_____

_____

_____

Date: _____ Topic: _____

_____

_____

_____

_____

_____

REFLECTIONS

Date: _____ Topic: _____

_____
_____
_____
_____
_____

Date: _____ Topic: _____

_____
_____
_____
_____
_____

Date: _____ Topic: _____

_____
_____
_____
_____
_____

Date: _____ Topic: _____

_____
_____
_____
_____
_____

REFLECTIONS

Date: _____   Topic: _____

_____
_____
_____
_____
_____

Date: _____   Topic: _____

_____
_____
_____
_____
_____

Date: _____   Topic: _____

_____
_____
_____
_____
_____

Date: _____   Topic: _____

_____
_____
_____
_____
_____

REFLECTIONS

Date: _____   Topic: _____

_____

_____

_____

_____

_____

Date: _____   Topic: _____

_____

_____

_____

_____

_____

Date: _____   Topic: _____

_____

_____

_____

_____

_____

Date: _____   Topic: _____

_____

_____

_____

_____

_____

REFLECTIONS

Date: _____ Topic: _____

_____
_____
_____
_____
_____

Date: _____ Topic: _____

_____
_____
_____
_____
_____

Date: _____ Topic: _____

_____
_____
_____
_____
_____

Date: _____ Topic: _____

_____
_____
_____
_____
_____

REFLECTIONS

Date: _____ Topic: _____

_____

_____

_____

_____

_____

Date: _____ Topic: _____

_____

_____

_____

_____

_____

Date: _____ Topic: _____

_____

_____

_____

_____

_____

Date: _____ Topic: _____

_____

_____

_____

_____

_____

REFLECTIONS

Date: _____ Topic: _____

_____

_____

_____

_____

_____

Date: _____ Topic: _____

_____

_____

_____

_____

_____

Date: _____ Topic: _____

_____

_____

_____

_____

_____

Date: _____ Topic: _____

_____

_____

_____

_____

_____

REFLECTIONS

Date: _____   Topic: _____

_____
_____
_____
_____
_____

Date: _____   Topic: _____

_____
_____
_____
_____
_____

Date: _____   Topic: _____

_____
_____
_____
_____
_____

Date: _____   Topic: _____

_____
_____
_____
_____
_____

REFLECTIONS

Date: _____ Topic: _____

_____
_____
_____
_____
_____

Date: _____ Topic: _____

_____
_____
_____
_____
_____

Date: _____ Topic: _____

_____
_____
_____
_____
_____

Date: _____ Topic: _____

_____
_____
_____
_____
_____

Chapter 7

Notes

They can because they think they can.

- Virgil (70-19 B.C.) Roman poet -

Chapter 7
Notes

This section is designed as a catch-all for all those items that may come up that do not necessarily fit into the other sections of your martial arts training diary. Here is a partial list of the types of entries made in this section by other martial artists:

☒ Important dates: belt tests, camps, special classes, seminars, etc.

☒ Phone numbers: classmates, instructors, equipment suppliers, etc.

☒ Order of belts: cost of tests, time normally at each belt, etc.

☒ Titles of recommended books

☒ Titles of martial arts videos

☒ Notes on specialized training: self defense, drills, etc.

☒ Students' names, classmates' names, instructors' names

☒ List of club/school fees and expenses

Supplement your Martial Arts Training

Without a doubt, the best way to improve or grow as a martial artist is to work hard, attend your classes consistently, and practice regularly on your own. However, sometimes you need something extra, an added shock to your regular routine that will stimulate extra growth for you as a martial artist.

The best way to stimulate extra growth as a martial artist is to go out and try new things. Get involved with new and different activities to supplement your regular martial arts training routine. These new situations will help you gain new perspectives and provide greater insight into your martial arts world, and, undoubtedly, about yourself.

Here is a starter list of suggested supplemental activities. Remember, the more new activities you try, the better you will become at discovering activities that will seem tailor-made for you:

- ☒ Observe a martial arts tournament.
- ☒ Enter a martial arts tournament.
- ☒ Attend a martial arts summer camp.
- ☒ Workout outside, at the beach, or in the mountains.
- ☒ Subscribe to a martial arts magazine.
- ☒ Read about a martial art or a martial artist.
- ☒ Learn about a different style.
- ☒ Have someone take photographs of you while training.
- ☒ Talk about your training with a senior student.
- ☒ Research some martial arts topics or problems.
- ☒ Have a party with some of your training partners or classmates and rent a martial arts video.
- ☒ Have a picnic with your martial arts class and their family members.

Slow Down . . . and Get There Faster

Once there was a Young Man who went to a martial arts master and asked him "How long will it take me to earn a black belt?"

The Master responded, "Three years."

The Young Man was impatient and asked, "What if I work all day every day?"

The Master responded, "Six years."

The Young Man pushed on and asked, "What if I work day and night?"

The Master said, "Nine years."

The Young Man was very frustrated and finally asked, "Why is it the harder I am willing to work the longer you say it will take?"

The Master said, "The answer is simple, when one eye is fixed upon your destination there is only one eye left with which to find the Way."

- Anonymous

Tanking Up: Keep from Running Dry

It is extremely important to keep your fluid levels up when exercising. It is especially important if you perspire heavily or if is hot or humid where you are training. Keeping properly hydrated enhances your performance. Letting your fluid levels get low is an invitation for disaster.

Drink before your workout. If you wait until you "feel thirsty" it may be too late and dehydration may have already begun.

Avoid drinks with **caffeine, alcohol, or carbonation.**

Cool fluids are absorbed more rapidly than warm fluids.

Drinking before working out is most important, and drinking during a workout is recommended. On average, most people need **8 oz. of fluid** for every **20 minutes** of training.

When working out vigorously for one hour or less, **water** is all that most people need to drink. If you want your water to be more interesting, you can add some fruit juice.

When working out vigorously for more than one hour, you want your drink to contain some **carbohydrates**. Carbohydrate drinks that contain more than 8% carbohydrate by weight tend to feel heavy and may cause stomach cramps. Heavily carbohydrated drinks and fruit juice should be diluted with 50% water.

If you have another physical activity later in the day, the best time to refuel your muscles with carbohydrates is one to two hours after the earlier workout.

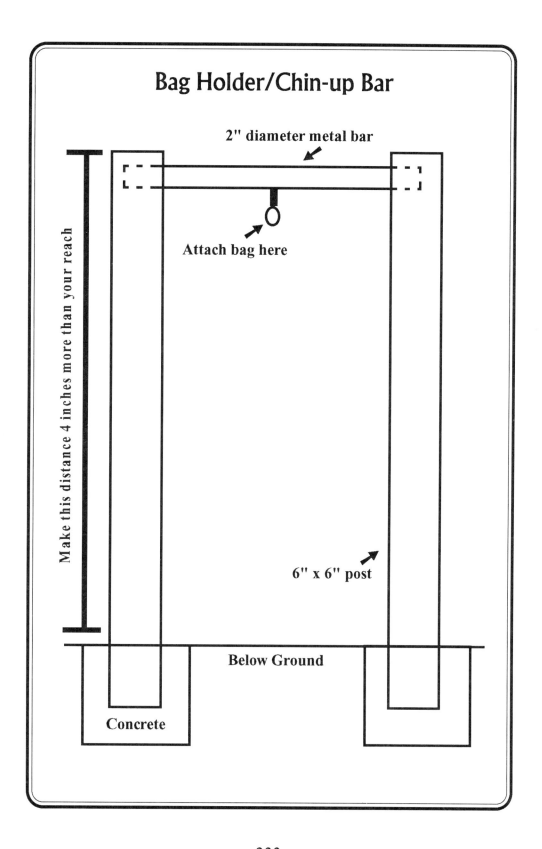

Bag Holder/Chin-up Bar

2" diameter metal bar

Attach bag here

Make this distance 4 inches more than your reach

6" x 6" post

Below Ground

Concrete

NOTES

Class times for Taekwondo:

    Mondays   6-7 PM

    Thursdays 4 - 5:30 PM

Summer tournaments

    Atlanta, GA - July 7

    New York - September 12

Children's classes - tests last week in June

NOTES

NOTES

NOTES

NOTES

NOTES

NOTES

NOTES

_____

_____

_____

_____

_____

_____

_____

_____

_____

_____

_____

_____

_____

_____

_____

_____

_____

_____

_____

_____

_____

_____

_____

_____

NOTES

NOTES

NOTES

NOTES

NOTES

NOTES

NOTES

NOTES

NOTES

NOTES

NOTES

NOTES

NOTES

Also Available from Turtle Press:

Teaching: The Way of the Master
Combat Strategy
The Art of Harmony
A Guide to Rape Awareness and Prevention
Total MindBody Training
1,001 Ways to Motivate Yourself and Others
Ultimate Fitness through Martial Arts
Taekwondo Kyorugi: Olympic Style Sparring
Launching a Martial Arts School
Advanced Teaching Report
Hosting a Martial Art Tournament
100 Lost Cost Marketing Ideas for the Martial Arts School

For more information:
Turtle Press
PO Box 290206
Wethersfield CT 06129-206
1-800-77-TURTL